# CRAZY
# LOVE

Other works by Pamela Uschuk:

Poetry:

*Finding Peaches in the Desert*
*One-Legged Dancer*
*Scattered Risks*
*Without the Comfort of Stars*


and numerous chapbooks

# CRAZY LOVE

**Pamela Uschuk**

San Antonio, Texas
2009

*Crazy Love* © 2009 by Pamela Uschuk

Cover art: "Red Ball" by Albert Kogel. Used by permission of the artist.

First Edition

ISBN-13: 978-0-916727-58-1

Wings Press
627 E. Guenther
San Antonio, Texas 78210
Phone/fax: (210) 271-7805

On-line catalogue and ordering:
www.wingspress.com
All Wings Press titles are distributed to the trade by
Independent Publishers Group
www.ipgbook.com

Library of Congress Cataloging-in-Publication Data:

Uschuk, Pamela.
  Crazy love / Pamela Uschuk. -- 1st ed.
    p. cm.
  ISBN 978-0-916727-58-1 (pbk. : alk. paper)
  I. Title.
  PS3571.S38C73 2009
  811'.54--dc22

                                   2009004224

*This collection is dedicated with ravenswoop and whitewater laughter to my favorite poet, friend and lover, Bill Root, to Julia Brooks for her music, to Teresa Acevedo and to Don and Lynn Watt for their enduring friendship.*

# CONTENTS

## FIGHTING THE COLD

# CRAZY LOVE

*O to be delivered from the rational into the realm of pure song . . .*

– Theodore Roethke

# THE HORSEMAN OF THE CRASS AND VULNERABLE WORD

*For Jim Harrison*

The hemlock loses the tanager,
a bright blood streak
in a whirling gauze of snow.
Where do we go?
You told me the eye was lost,
old lens in a dish of milk
going to blue-veined cheese,
a lens that sneezed
when you laughed the mockingbird's laugh,
the horse's white laugh,
saying your brother accidentally
shot it out as you crawled
under barb wire, hunting.

I was young and fell in love
with your wounds, your tongue,
half-song, half-glands,
strong as the Calvinist hands
that whacked and fed your swampy youth.
I was young and drank vermouth
while you fell to your knees
in the Ford's back seat where you teased
until I laughed too much
when you begged please,
and your one-eyed touch
stared up at the night jar sky,
blinked at Orion, your
archer, saying good-bye.

I laughed but I feared your tongue,
your thighs.  I was young.
I had heard.
Never love a poet at his word.

You were the man who could maim me
in those days when whiskey
clarified any dark thing.
Like Bobby and Annette we'd sing,
*Baby, you're my beach blanket;*
*I'm your Mickey Mouse coquette.*

You knew my crippled heart, my blind side
but I'd ride ride
ride on that edge where the heart's not given,
can't be taken
or lost to an archer or poet with one eye.
Oh, the heart has a spongy hide
believing in love's bromide.
Mine found its bed unmade, undone
when you left with your joking tongue.

But I tell you this now,
horseman of the crass and vulnerable word,
love is damp as a cloud-blown beach
and crawls in your bones
that never lose their ache.
When I dreamed your face—
so blindly polite, just the glimpse
of a lens of a face, just before
the horse, the dark and slippery horse I rode
so far out to sea
that the shore was a crumb the gulls couldn't eat—
I went numb in my sleep.
Even numbness passes.

I am half-blind in this half-blind night
but I've learned to ferment
wine from ash.
And you, it's always late—
you've broken your horse,
now lie under it.

# WITH ITS TOLL OF CHAR

*after hearing Ted Hughes*


All sounds bassoon in haze.
Trees stretch shoulder deep
in fog breathing up from the slow river,
where the courting of frogs booms
under the moon's waning halo.
To vague stars turning over sky, black limbs
hold up their devotion of autumn leaves.
Inside midnight's sleeve
the architecture of imagination slips
from its routine mooring
in an earthquake of dreams, and the car
jars you awake
as I skid to miss the fox
sniffing its mate dead on the freeway.

What shapes irony?  Coming home
late from the City after the Laureate's story
of the fox-faced man who peeked at him from the kitchen door,
then placed his charred hands over his poems,
I start at the overwhelming red tail
as it brushed the rushing bumper.

This fox is real.
It's dangerous, you say, to swerve
for animals caught on the ice.

Event becomes myth.  How
often we drift, safe in our faith
something will get us home alive,
though we risk everything.

Night gathers details we forget.
What it says comes true.

In fog, frogs never give up their insistent courting
and stars chart careful courses to dawn.

In the unkempt church of desire,
sometimes we pray for flame
that becomes its own fuel
charging the heart with its toll of char.

That fox must have watched his mate cross the pavement
like a stream parting their known woods
in the nightly routine of their hunt.
What he couldn't name split her side, flipping her once
as he snapped at the monstrous shape
even as it was swallowed wholly by dark.

The fox might have started sooner
from my oncoming car, but he stood
taking in her scent a last time
that commonplace night
none of us could any longer take for granted
as his red fur ignited, guard hairs
flaming spikes.

# MEDITATIONS BESIDE KOOTENAI CREEK

*for Bill*

## I

Sometimes I become what I least desire,
old as bone, uncomprehending
as the memory of pain.
Perhaps dusk comes into a room
and a woman rattles up
out of my throat, her eyes
empty as candles set aside for the dead
who no longer care for such light,
her flesh gone to the birds.
It is then
in gray light, she tells me
my skin sags, my heart is incomplete in its beatings.
I haven't learned to love
as much as the stars
who are at least not cruel.
Then, as if in a dream of fire along a foggy ridge,
I walk out,
hands sprouting green flames,
eyes not blind enough from blue smoke,
and I hear
from its sad shadow in wet grass
the sudden up-cry of a meadowlark
and I believe I will never be alone again.

## II

Listening to the wild applause of water
as it clarifies rocks we step across,
we hear what we'd name,

Western Tanager,
Song Sparrow,
Lazuli Bunting,
and over a silver patch of river, dim
in cedar shadows, the thick bilious
laughter of ravens.

You say,
*Walk in cold water.*
*Let it burn your feet.*

When you dive into the stream
you float for a while, then try
to hold the current in your pale hands,
and I remember your fingers
like coals stoking my breasts.

Your black hair waves like tentacles
or a negative halo radiant in its aquamarine pool.
Like blind minnows, your fingertips
bump the smooth skulls of stones underwater,
and, for a moment, I worry you'll drown.
But you rise, streaming
a chandelier of watery light
even our dark sides love.

Last night I dreamt of blood and beatings,
of giving away a bright red slip.
I tied my mother to a gypsy wagon and drove it West,
while her arms like kites
waved at passing weeds she blessed.  Over
and over she asked,

> *If the eye is blue as beach glass, will it*
> *see itself leap to the bottom of the stream?*

I watch a water ouzel now
whose name you won't believe.
It dips in and out of sizzling foam,
its thin yellow legs canny
on moss-covered stones I'd slip on.
I watch it disappear beneath white water
consuming itself above the bird
who emerges sky-gray, triumphant on the opposite shore.


## III


Ordeal by ice- -
      *twice, twice*
      *I'd change my heart to ice,*
      *suspend it twice in air*
      *to sprout wings for the wind's care,*
      *then cage it in the bones of flame*
      *to unlock the twins from separate names.*


Even as a young girl, I'd sit
beside a dry creek I'd wish was full
and sketch the tanager, shading
black wings on its heart-red sides.

Sitting alone under the vast
loneliness of trees in that small woods,
I heard voices huge with wind
and the coming dusk that wouldn't let me go.

Who could I tell but the dead?
What name could I give passion?
I watched the way animals surprised the grass
then I pretended I was a lion
no one could kill.

Summer's demise- -
*Gemini rises just before*
*midnight in the southern sky.*
*Castor and Pollux,*
*from icy toe to icy toe,*
*I'd trace with a twin's eye for balance.*
*Even the dead must have this simple joy.*


IV


After all these years, what we come to,
wet branches beating our chests as we wade
to the other side of the creek.
Reaching for the slippery knuckles of roots
clinging to clay banks, we fall
into water we can see through.
Cedar perfumes our numb fingers
that finally hold musky bark.
How deliciously we shiver.

This is the journey the heart makes,
back through water, under stars
filled with the certainty of submarine light.
We count the times we've drowned to live.

When I climb ashore, you splash
water straight into the air at my feet.
This time I can love and shove away the dead.
You splash again.
It is that simple.  I wait
for the ouzel to come back downstream,
wait for its small piping,
your splashing already deep inside me.

## CLIMBING DOWN
## FROM ENGINEER MOUNTAIN

*for Howie and Kate*

Descending to the trailhead at 10,000 feet
through meadows of insatiable wildflowers
as tall as you and me, through
the hot pink sleeves of paintbrush,
mountain bluebells, giant Angelica,
cow parsnip with its glacier blooms,
death camas, monument plants
stitched with waxy white flowers bees consume,
I stop and watch my friends grow smaller
as they walk ahead, thinking that this
is how an Incan mother must have felt
as she watched her children leave home,
hiking down slope and away from her
to the new shape of their lives,
their backs devoured by flowers,
dark heads bobbing like crows
as they disappeared into thick blossoms,
and it hits me that they will soon vanish,
return to their hearts' home in the East.

Already they do not miss me, don't
notice that I've stopped to turn over
the infinitesimal stars of the saxifrage
almost invisible at trail's edge, but
I know this pity is a stupid heroin,
clouding the way they congregate
in the parking lot looking up, waiting.

I want to reach out and hold my friends awhile
in the blue clarity of this altitude, make them fall
desperately  in love with sneezeweed
and coreopsis the color of absinthe,
with  the small gray teeth of talus
that clatter like broken crockery
displaced by elk above treeline, with my heart
that breaks at  each footstep swallowed
by wild  petals and retreating from the solitude
of ravens, from rock's passionate thrust
to the traffic  of what passes for the world.

# SUNDAY NEWS ON THE NAVAJO REZ

Stopped at a gas station outside Gallup, where
stray dogs circle the pumps for snacks from travelers, I fiddle
with the nozzle, and a white pickup pulls up.
The woman, my age, wrapped in a red Pendleton coat
tells me the obvious, *You have to pay inside first.*
*Since you want #1, I'll take #2.*
I thank her, embarrassed I am so punchy from
eight blown hours on the road from Tucson.

We pump together in pale winter sun. I like her soft face,
the way the turquoise squash blossom necklace
nestles like another planet between her lapels, and
I say something about gas being cheaper here
than in Colorado. She asks where I'm from.
She has a daughter in Fort Collins, across the state.

*Oh, you hear something about what happened up in Colorado?*
she asks. We trade what we know about the monster avalanche
that closed Highway 40. She repeats that her one daughter
is in Fort Collins, another in Phoenix, and the baby
at Fort Hood in the service.

*If my daughters were near that place, I'd be...*
her lips form the whispy syllables of missing
in her own language, a stiff breeze through tumbleweed.
She bows her head and mades a steeple
with the maternal fingers of one hand that taps atop her heart.

When I ask if she knows whether any people
were killed by the snowslide, she tells me,

*We don't have much time for news here,*
*what with the baby goats and lambs.*

*It's probably better to watch the goats.* I recall
this afternoon's report—3000 U.S. soldiers dead in Iraq.
Before I can say more, her voice drops
through my chest like a rock wrapped in black silk.
*One of our baby goats died this morning.*
*It was so beautiful.* For a moment I see
the kid dancing on its perfect hooves
in the irises of her dark water eyes.

*I'm sorry,* I say, but the words are clipped
as sparse grass in this land
of sandstone and wind.
They blow across the highway and into the path
of a semi heading north. When I start my car
I can see this woman lift each baby goat
in the cradle of her large arms and hold
it to the spot where her fingers
tapped out the names of her daughters, especially the last
ready to head out with her company
to a desert far across the unknown globe, where villagers
also raise goats and avalanches take the form
of a roadside waiting to explode.

# PLANTING TIGRITAS AFTER SNOW IN APRIL

Like a Lear jet out of control, wind shears,
slicing from Silverton ice fields, rattles
even indignant ravens from
the frigid chandelier of the blue spruce.
Down the block a goshawk blows like a kite
almost inside out in a gust
that thrusts its cold fists down my sore throat.

But I am an optimist, plant twenty-five
Tigrita bulbs, those open-mouthed lilies
I hope will roar near stunted tulips
and daffodils nursing bad self-concepts
refusing to bud. Mid-April
and still we shiver like the knock-kneed copper rose
banging our bedroom window.

Hard gardening here in the Rockies--
like tending the irregular seasons
of a long marriage, replacing rotted bulbs, adding
fertilizer to depleted earth, watering
frail roots and pruning back resentment
that blights healthy green leaves.

Take off your gloves.  Kneel
and claw open stony ground to loosen
dirt compacted by months of incessant snow
until each fingernail gleams like a saucy black moon.
Feel the shape of each root, the way it sucks
nutrients from mulch you pat around each tender shoot
to protect it against wind, hail, late killer frost.

By July your yard will be nothing
but a jungle of color so entranced, lightning
and thunder will only intensify
the muscular paws of these rearing tigers
you've coaxed from the cold shoulder of the world.

# DAKINI

*Hooked knife*
*Trident staff*
*Skull cup of blood*

Alone, I spin across the oak floors, small
galleon of unknowing.  I itch to phone
my husband, to hear
the honey blossom in his voice,
to erase all anger that would ever
snarl between us.  The angel of snow
pours out his skull across the yard.
There are no ideas in desire.  Even
the wind's longing
freezes chickadees  and nuthatches
to pine twigs.  Yearning taps
from the bottoms of my feet.
Two degrees and the snow creaks
like a hooked knife scarring wet slate,
screams like a skull in fire.

What they will say of me after my death—
she hid her heart in silver foil,
buried it in a raven's eye,
blindness beat and beat
on black wings for love,
all ways for love.

The weight of my hand on my arm
is the weight of an asteroid burning out
as it enters the atmosphere.  The weight
of loneliness is a wet feather
blown blue as ash across the drifts.

*Hooked knife*
*Trident staff*
*Skull cup of blood*

The triangle beneath my belly button
dances to flame. Trident tied with three
severed heads, knock from my skull solitude so loud
it could pass for drums until I empty
without being empty.

# WALKING IN SNOW
# ON A FULL MOON NIGHT

*for Happy*

White crunch of subzero
White moon spilling the bowl
of ewe's milk Celts drank
to celebrate this ewe's moon
halfway between solstice and equinox
White wolf lopes ahead
between white tire tracks
drifted and nearly lost
In profile, his head twice the size of mine
White silence of the husband
brooding over white
piano keys frozen between chords
of loneliness for the boy
scoring his heart
White paper waiting for words
to skate from the mind's revolving rink
White smell of Crisco
of white lard bubbling around eggs
of love love love with no red roses
strapped to its burning thighs
White stars blink
White Saturn raises the moon
White windless as frost
or the philosophy of ice riming the poet's cup
The senses are where ideas die
grateful as white moths into a winter sunset
White crunch of wolf paws
outleaping the deer trail
White wolf teeth take my whole hand
and for now
do not bite down

# CHRISTMAS DAWN

Five degrees and I slip
through the front door for kindling
when the click of the lock spooks
the buck just off the deck grazing on cheat grass.
At the edge of my sight, his hooves scatter
buckets of agitated gravel while I jerk
from all twelve prongs of his knife-tipped rack.

Two lopes and he stops, realizing
I am no dog or mountain lion, just
a slight woman in a shivering robe
skidding on frost and memories,
and he snorts to walk up for a better look
or to let me know he's boss.

I will always believe that he wanted to tell me
something essential about my life, but,
as usual, I fail to interpret what.
We stare at one another like lovers
with nothing left to say
or like parents whose mouths
suck the perfect zeros of goldfish
in the aquariums of their own isolation.

I am moved by frost in the buck's thick hair
around the bituminous depths of his eyes, the slick
black slits of his nostrils under antlers
that rise like a chandelier hooking sunrise.

I remember last night's dream
of flying back East to my teaching job

and the colleagues I'll never know, the way
we stare at one another pleasantly
and grouse a bit about overwork, lack
of private time, about sky
the color of tarnished tin foil, how we
really should get together sometime and talk.

Reassured by each other's silence, the buck nips
at frozen sage while I rummage the wood pile
for arthritic scrub oak twigs,
the cache of kindling
that, like iced  rhythm sticks
or bells,
              ring against the seasonal chill.

# CRAZY LOVE

Chickadees are most themselves, bravest of birds,
Blackfeet say, with the heart of a grizzly
booming inside their thin ribs.
My grandmother said,
*Watch out for small women,*
*the violin of joy that flexes inside their wrists,*
*their talent for making themselves*
*huge as Amazons.*

        Like all adolescents, I promised
myself happiness, an adoring mate. Got
clay guitars instead.
Thunder reigned and lips tore
from the thousand masks
in dreams. Lovers slipped away
like silk lilies lying to the wind,
and I dreamed I watched a dwarf build
an intricate toothpick pagoda at the end of a pier
jutting over the forehead of a black tossing sea.
The sky was the color of wet grapes
he slipped between his teeth.
Just as the dwarf set the pagoda
on fire, blazing the pier to my feet,
two giant turtles swam up
and carried me on their backs
across burning tide.

On the opposite shore, a chickadee buzzed, carrying
the wrist bones of a dwarf in its beak,
and I knew love couldn't be
far behind those small Amazon wings.

# RADHA LONGS FOR THE LION

At 6 degrees, the stars pour diamond thimbles
of frozen milk across blue snow.  I exhale
nebulas that crash to earth.
January and a lone elk crunches between pines.
Hunting season on mountain lions
just ended, but who can imagine the finger
that would pull that trigger,
finger blunt as a slap to a woman's face,
finger blind to beauty's soft mouth, to a flute's grace.
Flowers of ice blossom on my windows,
and I am grateful for this garden of cold.
Above the ridge, a lion dens deep in sandstone.
Her fur is the color of dried cone flowers, her breath
sky's blue mind.  I'll curl around
her thick and dreaming spine. When rifles
crack, I'll recarve their steel into jasmine vines.

# PEELING THE KITCHEN

Talk about exfoliation.  This archaeology will
take weeks.  First comes the ripping, then
total destruction.
                Wrenching out
nails with screeching crow bars,
we pry huge sheets of cheap paneling
from the old walls to reveal
the smoky history of paint, and under
        that, a century of wallpapers shed
like snake skins embossing rough sandstone.

Who chose the bottom pattern tattooed
with blue and red flowers or the pink sky
spackled with gold stars, tiny and multitudinous as fleas?
Beneath everything, the harsh ash-smeared
plaster is the logic that holds.

Like an argument that spirals out of control,
my husband and I cannot stop tearing.
                The white celotex ceiling
we've despised for years must go, so
with our bare fingers, we yank it
crashing, with its load of coal soot, onto our heads.

When the ceiling lies at our feet, what is there
but more dingy ochre paint, stars
blurred dusty as the distant Pleiades, a silver filigree
some wife may have chosen to mimic moonlight
bathing her spinning head while she sweated
over meals and dishes, waddled with her pregnant belly
between woodstove and table, where
her silver miner sat to slurp her rich soup.

Day after day, I mount the rickety ladder
to avoid my computer, where I should compose
poems that shake their fists at stars or hold
the fevered heads of children in distant warring lands.

It is comforting this peeling back,
the scraper prying up paint chips
the size of communion wafers
while I balance on precarious steps abrading,
the motion repetitive as prayer.

Where all the sweet conformity of yellow
          once soothed our kitchen, strange maps
of foreign planets bloom, a diasphora of galaxies
blasted into the variegated watershed of hearts
we can never really know.

Perhaps, this simple work is poetry, to strip
chaotic layers revealing the buried patterns
of our stories, charting
love's labyrinth, the way betrayal,
faith and fear spin us
in their webs, awful and light.

# HIT AND RUN

*We can't see. But feel some awful thing.*
*And we don't want to talk.*
*Doleful, the cry of eagle-owls, and hot*
*In the garden the wind is blustering.*

– Anna Akhmatova

# WHITE MOTHS

On diminished wind, tiny moths
white as thin dead lids
navigate sun's final rays.   What breathes between
horizon and night's full bloom—
bell of empty, then a sonic
boom scattering the far gone stars?

     As moths become the dusk, a fighter jet
rips the underbelly of sky, screaming
over the ridge.  On TV the surgical scar
grin of the President addresses the nation,
staying the course of war gone stale
as moth wings in his mouth, while
fresh from Baghdad, a slim line of flag-draped coffins
drifts down a Maryland conveyer belt
where, sun struck, they seem to flutter,
vanishing in flame.

## BUSHWACKED:
## LINES ON GLOBAL WARMING


Hopeless as swatting lies out of the White House
or trying to put out an oil field fire with a cup of water
is this war against the grasshoppers, who,
when I walk through weeds or rattle
the leaves on a pepper plant, leap
by the thousands to remind me
that power isn't always held by Goliaths
but by the numerous and persistant.
I've used up a quart of organic poison
the grasshoppers thrive on, sprayed them
uselessly with the hose, stomped
them into the deck, called them
wicked names they ignored
chewing mercilessly through perennials and broccoli,
sweet basil and jalepenos alike, shredding
even stringy giant white iris leaves
and stripping the raspberry to a single stem.
Monstrous gluttony, relentless destruction.
I suppose I could scream down
hatred from the sky on the idiot leaders
who voted against the Kyoto Accord, plead
with missing rain clouds
or throw up wailing hands and emigrate, but
I was born with that flawed gene
of never giving up. *Try try try
again*, as my mother said. Still
armored grasshopper faces are set
with awful grins of devastation—
those harpies of a vengeful god with his history of boils
and wrath. What's left
are ragged tomato plants

excreting their own foul scent
in this long season of wind
and sun, of wild fires and rainless nights,
thinning ozone and locust clouds
we continue to battle
as we do the plague of rhetoric
devouring the green of our lives.

# SEASON OF HEAT

*An eye for an eye makes the whole world blind.*

*– Mahatma Ghandi*

## I

I dream that, two by two,
a company of soldiers patrol
a river through a desert to the sea.
Gliding downstream, they navigate
crocodile-like, completely
submerged, but for their helmet tops.
They breathe water.  I can't see their eyes
or the enemy they seek.

Waking to BBC news, I confuse
them with another two US soldiers beheaded
in Iraq, retaliation dealt
from an endless deck of cards
in a game that's overstayed the table.

Revenge hisses the thousand names of hatred,
relentless as this season of heat
that tamps bear grass into a prickly yellow cot.

## II

For weeks now I've turned to gardening
instead of war, even though
I can't stop dreaming sweaty fatigues
and assault rifles, grim blue

barrels so hot from desert sun, they sizzle
fingerprints to angry welts.

I ache to bring them all home
but I know that, like my father and brother
after him, their passports have changed
nationality to the land of permanent damage,
one foot jerking from the adrenaline flash
of explosives, the other trying
to walk through the front door.

Next month my nephew leaves for Iraq.
How many coins can ever
pay for a heart or a mind?
His pregnant young wife writes
newsletters for Army wives,
each story upslanted as her beautiful smile,
despite shadows that deepen her son's
eyes, already missing his dad, who
waits at Fort Hood where mid-July steams,
humidity crackling with blue thunder, where
horizons are mirages shimmering like Humvees
patrolling the wreckage of Basra streets.


III


My dreams burn off with coffee, elusive
as fog exposed to sun.  I can't erase
the ruined smiles of those handsome dead GIs
or my nephew's wild profile
from my heart's album.
How many generations of faces
will be blasted
into the last charred snapshots of loss?

On the porch grasshoppers
assail pots of broccoli, sweet peppers,
cilantro and dill.
What was supposed to feed us
this winter is stripped by swarms
that chew everything as mindless
and methodical as insurgents
blowing up their own cousins
in Baghdad's broiling markets.

I soak the tomato plants, pack
new soil around their tough stems, then
switch the dial to classical music,
Vivaldi, hoping that, with enough water and
love, some of them will survive.

# CAREER MOVE

Dulled by office duties, the deadpan clutter
of my desk, committee e-mails with
no feet for rhythm, I doze like the weed-caked croc
offshore, watching for any slight stir
a furred foot dipped in shallows
might create.  In dreams I lick
the golden stomach of the girl I was
and the thigh of the woman I want
to be, each stretched like sand dunes
heaped by wind's sunburned hands.
I leak from each bureaucratic arrow shot
into hide that thickens over my heart until
no one hears the ruined thud inside
my chest, the need raw as ore
beneath earth's firm crust.
Whoever glimpses me in this buzzing swamp
might fear these yellow eyes
the electric tint of lemon sweat.  Look
closer and note how I take
lessons from a showy great egret, whose wings
benevolent as the courtesan's unfolding robes
reach up, then from
its warped reflection, lift.

# GEOMETRY LESSON

Just as the universe shifts to sketch
a new map of stars from the heart
of gasses bent around particles zapped
from black holes that would destroy them
so, falling in love, we invent lips
on the exact curve of the neck
most vulnerable to an axe handle blow,
lips unable to diagram a triangle of lies.

We outline the angles of hands
the way we'd sculpt our favorite dough--firm,
hot and slow.
Love we revise from the heart's disasters, knuckles
pounding the midnight door of fear,
the crazy laughter of flies that
        ferry betrayal on their jeweled wings,
even the ashes of our belief in our failure
to survive.  Love divides
or multiplies wet postulates of desire.

Foolishness and trust nuzzle
passion's womb.  Balance is axiomatic.
                Twenty years of falling in love
solves twenty years of hanging over the edge.
Twenty years of fire demand
twenty years of water to swell the flames.
What is the tender palm without the tough skeleton
forming the back of the hand
that can withstand both ice and unrelenting heat
as it calculates fault lines dictated by
what it can never see?

# MONEY CAN'T BUY YOU

Broke again and spending the last spare change
of aspen leaves rattling autumn sun, we set
back the hands of clocks, dreading
the black hammer of early nightfall, killer
frost and the stiff-legged horses who must go without
shelter save the bare arms of scrub oaks
all winter in the lower pasture.
Stupidly, I buy lottery tickets, getting
the numbers wrong each time, and
still my heart clicks like spring ice
breaking at the weekly announcement of winners.
I remember the poet back East, who asked
if we knew any good poets who weren't millionaires
in America, each word like a velvet fist
around our throats, accusing our lack. Of course,
his novel was chosen by Oprah so that his press
had to scramble to print enough copies
for the million fondling hands of TV worshippers,
and his back-woods boy face
lifted to cameras, to the sweet breath of fame
that began to line his pockets like sow's ears.
I sift through stacks of bills, a parfait
of debt, burying our kitchen counter, wondering
how to shift them from credit card
to credit card, that sure coal chute to destruction.
And, I stubbornly write verse
that has no fingers for profit, no nose
for investment, nothing but a gambler's heart
jumping on the river boat of promise,
of wax-winged and sun-struck hope
despite snow clouds eating the far mountains,
fat Canada geese laughing

over the backs of fenced horses,
flapping away from our toothaches,
thc astronomical cost of propane,
their wings the color of burnt coins, heading South.

# MOTORCYCLE ACCIDENT

*We're all tourists here.*

– Ernest Hemingway

Broken, the blue carapace crazed on pavement
tented by shadows, heaped under siren moan and hissing
flares.  Strewn across the dusk-wrenched street
those bloody souvenirs of final impact--
a blanket green as a sea anemone, motorcycle boot,
and smoking, the pickup that impales an elm tree.
Head swaddled, the dead biker is loaded by EMTs
into the ambulance. What speed can reimburse death,

fatal dents to body or pride?  I think of love's fights,
those head-ons of contrary like so many mountain goats
bleating as horns bash one on one to prove who
has power over who.  What souvenirs of wise
devotion will we leave, scattered like empty boots
for our kids to try on, what will we leave for good?

# HIT AND RUN

*for Stewe and Ingela*

If there'd been wind, the black
nexus of a hawk's eye refracting
a kaleidescope of blood, but
there was no wind, no blood, just EMTs
cracking the sternum of the shoeless young black man
sprawled on the berm while
traffic crawled like drugged beetles
around  him, just firemen's helmets,
yellow slickers and Sunday's impatient hands.
The soles of his feet were exactly our color.

If sun hadn't amplified all the fushia cheeks
of wild geraniums, the stiff tongues of protea
wagging from arthritic stems, had dust
not spun gold between the charred trunks
of African pines on Signal Peak, we'd have seen
even the brightest pigments ignore the broken
as they ignore our happiness.
Don't we all need
light, even though light  is
indifferent to everyone's grief?

If we hadn't been headed to the bluff
for wedding photos above the rippled blue
Atlantic, where Wright Whales sound,
no longer pursued by harpoons
for rich perfume, we'd never
seen the end of this man.
In the book of politics, poverty
is the last sin to die.

Who notices one more nameless death
these days.  He was someone's son.
At the scene, no police,
no culprit, just the beginning of rictus.
Whoever hit the young man is long gone
inside a coward's shoulder
turning  away.  There was, that day,
just the road and all of us climbing the mountain
and sorrow digging suddenly at the trees.

                              Cape Town, South Africa

# SELF HELP MANUAL

At my best, I am the eye of noon
staring beyond itself, worst, the updraft
of a Harris Hawk before it tucks
black wings to dive, severing
the pigeon's neck.
Sometimes I am as stubbornly habitual
as the pigeon shitting on rose leaves
and new laid bricks, beak clicking
like a broken watch on
a neighbor's sidewalk strewn with pesticidal seeds.
Other times I am dreamy as a wolf
checking its paws for spores
left by the failing Artic moon until
persistence hardens my will, and I become
that June bug banging into the autumn screen
that's outlived summer's need.

I will carve a guitar out of water, then
swim its length.
I will grow peaches on a grapefruit tree,
grafting limbs to shattered hearts.
I will chew blue glass until it releases
the captive language of stars.
I will lie, dig up the sewer leading to
a sticky drain, learn the clogged pipes
of hatred, of scorn, then
flush them clean.
I will be more gullible, believe
the horizon when it shouts
*light*! I will be the torture rack
that stretches out my own truth.

BELL NOTE

*for George Uschuk*


A bassoon dropped to the bottom of Lake Michigan
your voice returns in the rain that reduces the world
to amorphous cold smoke I cannot shape.
Shape was never indistinct in your hands that
sculpted everything from kitchen cabinets to built-in beds
and writing desks; those fleshy lathes as
tough and heated as steel poured into molds
for car frames you lifted at the Olds, where you
put in more years than I have teeth
to bite through the stinging barbwire of loneliness
that binds my heart.  I recall Sunday
morning phone calls, our bad singing
and your war stories better than any church-
bound sermons, laughter huge as any savior
that brought me back from tightrope walks
across those myriad ice bridges of self-doubt
swayed by disillusionment's raw wind.

Sometimes, Dad, there is no loneliness
like an ad for the Superbowl,
all those coach's blunders you'd cuss out
or the lies of politicians on TV
smiling as they staggered like possums
on the sides of reason's highway.

Remember driving cross-country year
after year from Michigan to Colorado, the Cutlass
a waxed pendulum ticking to the rhythm of your stories—
the way Johnny Weismuller taught you to swim
in ninth grade or the time you flew the bomber
all the way across the Atlantic from Brazil

to the coast of Africa, spread gold
as a lioness against a gigantic wash of blue—
stories to keep each other awake
as we sucked orange wedges, licked
Snickers bars from our fingertips
numbed on the humming wheel.

What did you say to Mom, who sat
knitting or reading in the back seat, when
she'd startle like a rock dove, head
jerking up at us with her shriek,
"We're going the wrong way!
That field's on fire.  It's heading
right for us!"  Maybe her delusions knew that
the fire was always heading for us, her heart,
that you'd always keep her from the flames.

Today is your birthday, Dad, and what heads
for me is memory's long smolder
damp as campfire coals
on a star-spidered Michigan beach
where somewhere offshore your voice bells
from its submarine cave
my forgotten loved daughter's name.

# RAFTING THE RIVER OF DEATH

*for Joy*


At current level, we floated on a piece of tin, some thin
metal Texaco sign given to us by gods we couldn't see
to keep us dry and eye to eye with the drift of the dead—

dismembered whales, dolphins, polar bears and oceanblown
birds, chopped up and overtaking us in the river
pouring from the base of Alaska.  The known wilderness

was skinned of trees, plundered beyond dreams.  Like
a crazed ice floe, the eye of a whale and its nebulae
of surrounding flesh whirled close enough for us to see

the vast intelligence dyed into the paralyzed lapis nexus.
At first, I was repulsed by the span of man-centered carnage,
massacre, the demise of wildlife on such a Grand

Old Party scale, but your eyes told me how sacred these parts
and beautiful.  You said, *touch them.  It is all
touch.*  So I reached across heartbreak to stroke the eye

beyond corruption, my hand a neon wand of fear, my heart
spasmodic in its bell of loneliness.  Perhaps it was then that I
could join the dead or was simply comforted by communion,

touching the whole mouth of creation breathe into each
separate cell, a being indivisible as the universe
or the knowledge of love.  I knew, then, no one is immune,

no oil exec or lumber emir, secretary of war, you
or me, knew that our spiral wires are constructed from
the DNA of twinned stars and bonded like quarks

or hydrogen molecules, interdependent as electricity
and balancing everything.  In that iceflash recognition
I knew why we'd chosen to ride out  destruction

on such a precarious wing, why there is no safe shore
to keep us untouched witnesses,why our charge
is the constant navigation of song through dreamdeep currents

braided with islands of beauty, of terror, betrayal, passion
and fear.  Call it mystery or logic. It is all
the same.   Death is what we misname.

# THE EGYPTIAN ROOMS

*for Joy and Audle*


Who can separate the paired falcons, memory
from imagination, can split the sky.
Too close to flesh tone, I never liked pink stone,
especially granite with its graphite veins
like the varicose headstone on my grandparents' grave.
This museum altar crowds other
displays to the edges of the room.   Stroking
its sacrificial trough, electric
as forbidden skin, once again I'm hurled back.

Our black eyes were shaded
blue, novices raised in the same temple room.
Gold ringed our necks, ankles,
our bird-boned wrists. We laughed at
our chests unflattening themselves.

At desert noon a falcon screamed
just before the priest
carried in his bitter pack of leaves
to slip between our teeth.
When he lifted his white robe
for the stiff initiation, my foot
refused with a perfect kick.
Anger like white knuckles
tightened his face as he shoved
the knife through my terrified ribs.
I'd tell you it was painless
beyond the blade. For you
the room ached like a split womb.

How much of memory is will?  We are still
the same laughter, bodies
slim as deer, story-telling
fingers ringed by shields—
                silver, lapis,
turquoise and gold—
with their histories of wounds and needs.

How often have we died young, sacrificed
for love or lust?  Sometimes
I dream wide, of a river ripe with crocodiles
or a lion deciphering the dusky musk of reeds.
Who would believe
the asteroids of desire
that whirl in my sleep?

This morning when you dizzied in the staggering space
between skyscrapers on the way to the Met,
I heard them speak.

Now all of it rockets back—
how my dead flesh married stone
while you laced the jade frog
on the leather thong around my neck.
Tears worried your angel dark face
searching for my voice that thinned
above the altar where I never learned to pray.
Inconsolable days you arranged
orange trumpet flowers in my hair
until your tears were blades
that sliced the priest's drugged throat.

Two thousand years later we enter this passage way
lined with mummies behind glass.
Their anger bites the hemostatic air.
I can almost see them breathe.

Who's to say which catalogue
of sacred wounds is real?
Furious for balance we lean
against one another's temporary form.

You hold your hand over the songbird
of your heart tossing in terrible wind.
Hold onto me when we return
to the traffic-jazzed streets,
the blind blotters of skyscraper windows,
all the rushed faces who won't meet our eyes.

We are dangerous, hot
as smuggled knives.  How short
the time.  We are smoke
from funeral flames, rising
cold and pure as the language of stars.

# WE THOUGHT
# NO ONE
# COULD SEE US

*To hold on: that's everything.*

– Miroslav Holub

## LAUNDRY LIST
## ON THE BACK OF A MAPLE LEAF


After the eclipsed moon's full howl, how
strange the plunge and lift of autumn
temperatures that mimic the knees
of a girl first testing ocean surf
with her perfumed feet before
her headlong dive to end her dreams.
Flame takes the sky
on the last Indian summer wind
reeking of diesel
from construction across the street,
a fire ant wind biting us
to believe we've flipped
the calendar of our hearts back to June bugs
and a chigger-clogged sun, except
we can't miss the branches
as bare as our longing to hold
this warmth against ice rains
that will maim us, freeze
our joints, shatter
our sex inside
their teary rictus.
                    Frost's rigid fingers crack
the lips of fall dawn
just as sun snaps like a black seed on fire
over the horizon and the blue heron unhinges
its death-colored wings.
This could be the last day on earth,
day rung by rusted clappers of goodbye,
the salt of loneliness smeared
down time's crenellated spine,
a dog regarding the Vet's needle

that will put her down, the last cry
of the premature lamb
secured in the coyote's teeth,
crocodile smile of the lover
planting his betrayal in a handful of dirt,
a chipped tooth of grief.
In window urns and gardens
all over town, winter cabbages
replace the last defiant blooms.

Winston-Salem, North Carolina

# NOTHING BUT SOUTHERN

*for Teri Hairston*

*I am not happy*, you sway like a bear
at an empty hive. Shaking
the health conscious oatmeal cookie
inches above your coffee.
*This doesn't have nearly enough sugar.*
The vending machine is out
of honey buns, and gloom takes over
your sweet tooth's afternoon.
*I am nothing but Southern,* your voice glazes
the humid air compressing the office,
and I laugh.  My accent is clipped sage
next to the deep espresso yours pours
to jazz even the dullest duty
as we bend over budgets and endless press
releases we'll send before five.
Sometimes we sneak off from the four white walls
of the institution we serve like we did last Friday
when Mars loomed like the clarified eye
of an Amazon, closer to Earth
than it has been in 60,000 years.  At midnight,
we floated in a rich man's Olympic pool
while he slept, and we became
our own true animals craving what's sweet,
two bears and an antelope
whirling in night's indigo tea.
My grizzled love twirled me,
a compass needle homed to the steady red gleam
as you paddled, dark calves glistening like slick fur,
your laughter deep as a raven's wing beat,
and we forgot for a moment the centuries of slave blood

that fertilizes this southern soil, blood
of your grandmother, blood
of your grandfather, the way
that skin color still chains the passports of the world.
Mars gave up its mean battle gear
in the sugary arms of late summer,
and while the rich man you take care of slept
we wrote a  new history
carried in the cool stream of the Milky Way,
licking the honey of delight
unchained.

# NORTH CAROLINA GHOST STORY

*for Elizabeth Dewberry, Teri Hairston and Zelda Lockhart*

I

Sunrise torches the Winston-Salem Projects,
a saxophone of light swelling the cups of red buds
and crenoline skirts of Japanese cherry blossoms
morphing my back yard from orange clay
to Southern belle parfait that a red-tailed hawk cuts
through chasing pigeon breakfast on the wing.
Spooked, the blue jay creaks, a rusty gate
flapping as it navigates dogwood's white dance.
I walk to campus, hear a rustle,
see how the small things of the world survive.
A burrowing chipmunk pokes his nose
from rotten old magnolia leaves,
breathes sky.

II

I think of my friend, Teri, waking
in the Hood, her dreds emerging
from a thrift store blanket, waking
to pigeons she feeds strut and coo
on the fire escape, waking to
sirens and the smell of grits and coffee
from across the common lawn.

I remember her eyes last night,
chilled even while she laughed,
*I don't want to hear about ghosts. Black girls don't*
*like ghosts; don't tell me about no ghosts, uh, uh.*

So Teri waited in the damask parlor
of the elegant old college President's house
while we three climbed secret stairs
to the attic, where dusky air
compacted like a punctured lung
with each step until our chests squeezed
into the small wheezing cry
of the girl we all heard dragged
across the floor to the terror of her life
and we felt her die
and die and die, her fear bright
and palpable as blood
that streaked her thighs.

None of us could speak but
strained to translate the acid etch
of tears unredeemed, the mystery
inside the marred grain of the oak floor,
but we couldn't in our strictest scholarly logic
tame the icepick panic
chipping at our own hearts.

Then I whispered what earlier I'd seen —
the vapor trail of the matron
corseted in grim gray muslin,
a living cauldron of grief
boiling through the rooms downstairs,
clouding wallpaper, pink
and oblivious as a bouquet of carnations.

Was she looking for a daughter, hers, her maid's?
We left the muffled screams of the attic floor,
stained so deep two pine boards had to be replaced
long after the Civil War. We left
with no real clues, just the urine reek
of terror leaking from the walls,  the long echo

of screams beating like small fists
or an arrhythmic heart,
a temperature drop
none of us could shake, even when
we descended to the parlor and Teri's quip
about *the questionable ethnicity of Spectral Americans.*


## III


Accompanied by the sweet flutes of Carolina wrens
I unlock the President's house
to clean up last night's party, wondering
about the school's boast of its underground railroad,
and how those who began this school had kept slaves.

I scan portraits decorating peppermint walls—
the magnolia blossom faces of gentlemen tobacco barons,
plantation owners who never pulled
a boll from a plant.

Back from the hunt, one gent leads
a dapple grey thoroughbred
to the livery's whitewashed stalls, his fox hounds
splayed helpless as contorted cutouts
behind the thick black hooves.
The man's face is pinched, his thin mouth
locked on lust's hard verb,
eyes ashy, vest cinched tight
under the black waistcoat above white jodpurs
highlighting the bulge between the tops of his thighs,
the mahogany blur of a young girl
escaping around the corner
of the elegant white house, up the steps
just out of our sight.

# CHERRY BLOSSOMS ON SALEM AVENUE

Frail as the lace veil on Aunt Hazel's Easter hat,
cherry blossoms whoosh across pavement
the homeless Vet shuffles over
on his daily pass past my house.
He argues with wind, raises one
grimed finger to mockingbirds diving at his head.

I remember Aunt Hazel's warning
never to give myself to boys
who would surely ruin my first and precious flower.

Cherry blossoms rustle papery tambourines
peevish at the brown-bagged bottle
the Vet lifts to his lips with his one good arm
the way rude wind lifts
the crepe skirts of those maiden blooms.

Does the Vet whose wounds no longer matter to the sky,
smell the cinnamon of the pink carnation
he once pinned to the peach-chested girl
he  asked to the Prom, now the soccer mom
and NASCAR wife with kids of her own
who revs past in a Lexus, silver
as cold Yankee rain, silver
as a land mine cover,
a metal skull plate?

# LEAVING CHATTANOOGA

*for Rick Jackson, Bill Mathews and Regina DeCormier*


Big as Bubba, the fat black lab, and slick
                            as an oil spill off the Galapagos,
catfish hover in the aquarium of early morning goodbyes
as we board the shuttle for Atlanta with its mockingbirds
and traffic jams of white peach blossoms, magnolias
thrusting red-fisted buds from tough  shells
like the chapped hands of children
stretching through barbwire
in Afghanistan or Dachau.

Over dinner late, Rick's face flamed
when he told us that visitors aren't herded through
barred gates into Dachau the way prisoners were
but that they file through a tourist door
and the first things they see aren't crumbling shoes
or starved spoons but a huge billboard
advertising condos with a view of the camp.

Angry blades of light sliced from Rick's feet
as he trudged through gas chambers, rusted
showers and creamtoria that stank like singed hair
even after fifty years of cameras, coca cola,
granola bars and beeping cell phones
that file through the gift shop to buy postcards
embossed with stacks of bones, wheelbarrows
bloated with loads of bodies, the
pinched faces of children, rooks
beaten into their ragged feathers by hatred's ice rain.

Who would send those kinds of postcards
anyway?  Wish you were here.  Love
and torture thick as tear gas or goodbye.

Aboard this bus, the tires tick like fingernails
against a grenade, and I think
how the list of dead friends stretches
its skin into a yellow lampshade glowing with grief.
Rick misses the heart of Bill Mathews, reciting
Petrarch over laughing glasses of Chardonnay.
And a solid year of Good Fridays can't begin to atone
for the memory of Regina's defiant pulse
stopped in its lonely wheelchair.
I see her hands shimmer like blackbird wings
lighting the last cigarette of poetry, rattled
blue as the hoofbeats at her door.
Sometimes I am slammed
by the rain-soaked ventricle of gone.

I try to leave those I love long before dawn
so goodbye can't pull on its hiking boots, so it will be
too tired to rip bones from my wrists
or pull the teeth from stars setting
beneath the arrhythmic horizon of tires on rainy pavement.
It never works,
                    but the sky this morning is dark and gracefully
monstrous as a catfish sinking through the silt of a river
                    I don't know how to name.

# LOVE NOTE ON A MONDAY MORNING IN NORTH CAROLINA

*with apologies to William Carlos Williams*

Off to the airport again, you sail
away from home as you do each week,
owl-headed Odysseus bound
for the island of sorcery and soaring glass,
where a bear could be turned into a pig
on Times Square if he didn't watch his back.
This is just to say that there are black plums
ripening for you in the pewter bowl on our counter.
As if they could atone for the sin of separation,
the dogs hang their heads
in the baskets of their lonely paws
while I wait for you in the buttery sheets
of my suspended breath, figuring
balance on the tightrope of our dreams
without fear in air humid and alien
as rainy tarmac you now land on.   Stride out
into the concrete labyrinth, break
open the full bear bouquet of your life, know
the thread is strong that will lead you home,
where the plums are bursting their skins.

## SAVING THE CORMORANT
## ON ALBEMARLE SOUND


Chill mist defines the dawn world
as we paddle for the Great Dismal Swamp
past the ghosts of drowned cypress.
I focus on a pair of cormorants a hundred yards offshore.
One startles skyward eaten by fog
as its mate slingshots up then slams
back, leashed to the gray chop.

Who would stake out a bird
to drown in rising tide?
To set it loose we paddle hard, not considering
the problems salt wind and two wolf-dogs pose,
noses testing sea scents from mid-canoe.

Fog silent we glide near enough to see
the net hung with irresistible underwater jewelry—
fat sea bass flapping against polystyrene
crosshatching the bay.
Diving through tea-colored currents even
the cormorant's keen night sight failed
to detect plastic's fatality, and we wonder
how much we miss beneath surfaces.

When you lean to free the snarled bird
big as a goose, the screeching orange beak
and terrible machine gun slaps
of its one free wing whack your hand,
shoulder, your unprotected head.

Both dogs leap wild, and we rock,
nearly pitch into frigid surf.

Over the heave of my heartbeats
I hear our screams for the dogs of fear
to lie still in the bottom of the boat.

Each time you reach over the bobbing gunnel
slicing a tough link with a small fillet knife,
that hooked beak strikes, tattoos you
through your thin leather glove
until you grasp the muscular neck.

We are as precarious as we've ever been.
If we swamp, we'll freeze
before we can make shore, but
neither of us was meant to quit. Those
set-jawed wills that hopelessly mire us
in arguments, here bite through
panic knotting up our chests.

While you struggle not to hurt the frantic bird
I inch the canoe bow to a punky cypress trunk
that threatens to disintegrate.
How can I not think doom as I hug this
illusion, just another wrong choice
that crumbles in my hands?

Holding the netted now aloft, you hack
strand by strand, and with each slash
the cormorant thrashes, tangling deeper in the gill net
until we all assume an unnatural calm.

Numb and saturated by spray, it is now
I love you most, love your thick purple wrist
straining to hold the bird above hungry waves,
love the deft gentleness of your swollen hand
that cuts brutal knots without wounding the bird
who stares at you resolute as its barbed restraint.

When, finally, through the last
styrene twist, you fling the huge bird free,
it tucks oil black wings to dive deep, then
surfaces twenty feet out to regard us, before
plunging for the murky heart of the Sound.

We are stunned as any congregation touched
by near calamity, saved like that bird
putting watery distance between itself
and us as we paddle back to shore
above the condemned rows of sea bass and all
those snared in darkness we'll never see.

## ANOTHER WIFE SEES HER LOVE OFF TO WAR

I'm not surprised I sliced my finger
after you left this afternoon.
The moon rises in its full fog of longing,
and I hear a vibrato of goodbyes like grenades
going off under my skin.  In my purse
your cell phone takes messages
you won't hear for months.

My words walk into dreams
rattling their ankle cocoons that recall
the sweet tremble of wet wings
before they learned to fly.  Now you fly
thousands of miles from my heart
that flutters off from the stench of its duties
to keep blood and bone alive, swollen
by an ache as acute as winter stars
driven under my fingernails.

Some cosmic joke this passion that strips
my skin to flap like prayer flags
in the complete loneliness of snow.
What can melt ice when men drum
for revenge, and I am stuck again
in the swamp of their rhetoric, their need
to maim the long arms of desire?
A compass needle spun in the palm of history,
battles come true in grief's key of screams.

What skirmish do I need when my heart is set
to leap into the pyre of its longing, dreaming
fat as the moon that remembers the skin tent
flapping like hawk wings in desert wind,

the spin of me dancing before you ride off
with your warriors, the last tattoo
of your fingers, text message on my cheek?

# WE THOUGHT NO ONE COULD SEE US

Although it didn't freeze, the tulip tree flames, its
leaves as big as fiery umbrellas
plunging to the neighbor's late lawn, and I see
for the first time all summer, holes
in our privacy.
            The illusion we've loved, that
we're alone and secret in the woods, instead
of backed up like a truck full of contraband
to a dull suburban development,
begins to unravel as we tilt away from sun.

Across the road, horses graze on humid grass,
neighbors we adore.  They drift
like contented ghosts through morning fog
almost distracting us from the NPR commentator
who breaks news—in Fallujah our soldiers
have gunned down another Iraqi police squad
by mistake, police our forces trained
to rein in the chaos of our war
on terror.
          *Friendly fire*, the military names
this massacre of all eight officers, just like
the massacre of nameless scores
these months, although *friendly*
crashes like a mortar through the airwaves,
shatters the floor of the helpless kitchen we pace
while we wonder how we can paste all
those dying leaves back on our trees.

# FIGHTING THE COLD

*Some women wait for something*
*to change    and nothing*
*does change*
*so they change*
*themselves.*

– Audre Lorde

# GRAY SUNRISE

In high desert, fog is the immigrant
that slips in like my grandmother did
as a girl at the turn of the last century,
drenched in its wool coat of gray mist
and speaking a soft-syllabled language as it crosses
the weather border this morning
to enlighten everything with grays.

Sometimes we need brute change, the throat
open to chill even as it sings into its new life
far from any recognizable home.  The rare appear
at the feeder—Lazuli buntings,
black-headed grosbeaks, the one
rufous-sided towhee with its simple request
for tea.  Even the raspberry
seems to grow new limbs overnight
and the stump-tailed bully of a cat analyzing
what lives in the culvert, tunes its ragged ears
to hear water's softer whisper.  We wait for the burnoff
and wonder at those who daily wake
to this ground-bound cloud bank—
how easy to hide inside what could kill you—
we whose skin and eyes are scalded by glare
so intense, it reveals what we'd sometimes rather forget.

So it is with poetry—whether to pen syllables that shout
finally from my grandmother's tongue
as she holds a broken milk bottle to
my grandfather's throat that threatens another beating
or to seek obfuscity in images whose hazy hands
are their own magicians, pulling peace roses

and wren song from the top hat of imperfections—
to walk into what shifts
between a world mist-distorted
and one incinerated
by light.

# CHANGE OF HEART

*For Val*

The cliché is transparent as beveled glass.
You hold your hand to the spot
the doctor shocked to death to stop tachycardia
galloping like a steroid-pumped stallion of misery
through your terrified chest.

A change of heart after half a century, and
you didn't know how still it could sound
in your throbbing head, still
and sweet as the moment before dawn.

They call it a heart ablation
and they no longer split the ribs but slit
the femoral artery to insert wires
snaking to electrify the four chambers of your being.

Would you tell me, then, if you saw
ghosts or the light of memory
we share strung out in a circulatory system
penetrating each of us?

"You hurt my heart," you complained,
sitting straight up despite deep anaesthetic
when the doctor zapped the spot.
What delineates delusion from miracle?

The tears on your face tell me more
than any surgical report, more than the rerouting
of blood flow from the weakened artery,
a birth defect no one detected until you were fifty.

How does the blood know
to chart tides of sorrow and joy
as if these twins are inseparable from birth?

What I know is that
it is never too late for repair,
to change hearts damaged by the conjunction
of those whose parenting hung around their necks
like collars of need.  No, it is never too late
for a malformed heart to create
a new pathway, opened, loved.

# BLOSSOMING IN LILITH'S GARDEN

I pick wild cherries plump as the fire moon
as I brush through
my garden's full blooms—
            fuchsia petunias that tongue
velvet Pasque flowers pulling themselves
erect as silk temples next to the blousy lips
of giant snapdragons, pink
cosmos in gauzy frocks, and
red geraniums lewd on green stalks.
Sky flaunts blue skin spread
wide as Lilith, Salome, and Bovary in their prime
opening luscious arms to lift
golden eagles, ravens, mountain
blue birds and vultures alike.
This heat-ticked season shouldn't be wasted.
I listen for love's slow snores
storming our house and know
I want to be entered the way wind
bites into wildfire crackling through sage
or the way the sunset-bellied brook trout
strokes her entire body into the muscular current
to find upstream. Earth longs for torrents, for
rain's unbound knuckles
to pound jazz into it after months of sun.
And me? Today I am Lilith
open as a garden where insolent fruits
and heavy-breasted flowers shake their booty
above the snaking roots of trees.
Wrapped in a silk robe the color of wind
I pad inside from the barefoot yard, fertile
soil splaying my toes, wild cherries
staining my teeth.

# ADULT ORTHODONTICS

For beauty, I had four healthy teeth pulled,
and each morning since I spit blood
pooling like regret's venom
at the back of my throat, wondering
why I wanted all my life
a straight smile.  Sure
the drift of years tugged all the front biters
to the left and the molars bent
like supplicants in toward the tongue
so that I chewed on the thrust up edge
of the right side, but haven't I always lived
on the edge with my bad enunciation,
a rebellious overbite?

In college I was sent to a speech therapist
who could not manage to create
around my uncooperative teeth
the perfect s or delineate an f
without the whistling music that waltzed
between the gaps.  She gave up,
handed me a sheet of exercises that I soon forgot
in lieu of how to keep boyfriends
from running off with girls whose canines
were tamed to round, less prone
to tear into chunks of bright red meat.

For beauty, I worked out, lifted
weights, ran full-out miles,
capped a stray tooth,
tried various mascara tints, dyed
my lips the color of a fresh stab wound,
then finally landed a real job and learned

to smile without exposing those strong
and wolfish fangs.  Now, in the mirror
it is absence I see, four clots
like black lakes of angst in my gums
and what I will have gained
when the metal cages are gone—
a smile straight out of Vogue,
white, unwild,
vegetarian.

# SMALL ODE TO WINE

Begin with Beaujolais, that certain slant of light
through eagle's blood, best with new lamb.
On May evenings, when apple blossoms beg
for heat, tango in the young arms of Beaujolais.

At broiling August dusk, grill fish, then
uncork Pinot Grigio, citrine and frail as lingerie.
While you sashay across the moonbricked patio,
it will cool everything but your hips.

With heavy winter beef, cabernet
strikes the palate electric as the eye of lust,
dark as the tongue of a wet jaguar
sliding the length of a woman's thigh.

Oh, Lord, those red wines have legs
thick and muscular as Bacchus or Pele
to kick all memory to smithereens, click
back the ticking clock, but it is the good dry white
with its small hands tucked inside your cheeks,
that adores your dizzy face.

# EIGHTIETH BIRTHDAY

*for Ella Marie Uschuk*

Eighty.  Mom, I can hardly believe
the roundness of the number,
a fat ant body or ice-skate track of time, how
it always brings us back
despite irony, love or distance to where
we started from, the curve
of the fetus in the womb, arms
pinned to the sides by amniotic fluid or stroke,
fish mouth cocked open gulping air.

I didn't send you a birthday card.  I drew
an iris for you in my head
but it never made it to the paper,
I picked yellow roses.  My ghost arms
hugged your shoulder blades veiled by blue skin.

My heart is a huge womb of grief
when I think of you curled, a comma of skin
stretched over bone, in a hospital bed this long year
and a half,  how your mind howls like a coyote
in a desert terrorized by memory.

Does the white cat still stalk your bedclothes,
bloody buffalo rise from the tiled floor?
I remember the china fragility of your creased forehead
under my lips, the iron stubble of your hair
whirled like those English fields by crop circles
at the back of your head where it dents the flowered
                                                    pillow,
your sea green eyes tuned skyward.

What do I remember at the bottom of the loop?  The time
you fashioned the magician hat, a paper cone
with a blue scarf sewed on
for a veil I refused,
                    and I was ten
and stupid enough to want something else.
The yellow slew of roses you snipped each June
to celebrate your easy short labor,
my tiny face at your breast.  The way you carved
gardens, Canterbury bells blue as exhausted lids,
bright lipstick-colored peonies,
the brash solar explosions of gloxinia
and deep velvet tongues of snapdragons
from losses that accrued each year.

Death drove your shoulders, but refused
to take you on the road all those you loved
sped down so prematurely.  What's fair
in a universe that pinned your spirit
wriggling on its mounting board of fear?

Eighty, Mom, you're eighty and your mind
caroms like shrapnel shattering time.  Eighty, dear Mom,
and there's nothing to celebrate but love from the daughter
who was never good at numbers or good-byes.

# HOUSE CLEANING

*for Judi and Val*

1

How comforting the animal suck
of the vacuum that creates order from
the chaos of a bad news call
in the middle of the night.
                              Upright
Kirby or Electrolux pulled like a Conestoga
on rubber wheels, it doesn't matter
as long as the hose lies cozy as a lifeboat oar
        locked in the hand
that scans a hardwood floor for dust motes
or nuzzles into the deep nap scalp of wall to wall.

2

My aunt hated housework, disdained
the vacuum's grinding grizzly roar rattling her earrings,
interupting her daily soaps so
we were afraid to eat in her house, once stepped
over a dead dog, my cousins said
was sleeping on the barn floor.

3

I knew a woman who swept her floor naked, bosom
shaking like two jumbo bags of oatmeal
as she laughed *It's my house, damn
it, and anyone who doesn't like it can
always get married.*

4

Before their divorce, my sister's husband
bought a carpet cleaner, the *Green Machine*, became
obsessed with getting out the deeper dirt
in Berber carpets he'd installed, spent
weeks shampooing and sweeping
instead of writing blues songs
that rang inside memories of his father beating
the tempo of anger into his head.


5

The times my mother's mania
dilated the red tide in her eyes, then
hissed like a distempered throat,
she wailed day and night and lost
the urge to clean anything, so us kids learned
housekeeping as a manual to save our lives.
We scrubbed and swept and polished until
there was no visible evidence of her neglect.


6

Grandma kept her house immaculate
as the lilac-laced handkerchief she stuffed
in the hip pocket of her housedress.
I remember galvanized buckets of rainwater
she collected to wash her silver hair, the lemon
smell of oak and mahogany
after she dusted. She advised, *Don't work*
*as hard as I did. Scrubbing floors*
*bends your back like birch. Follow*
*what your heart says.*
*Dance.*

7

Before my mother died, we bathed her, washed her hair, slipped on her best orange flowered dress, ruby ring, pearl necklace. My sister carried her comatose to my newly-washed car. I drove and all three of us daughters teased one another as if we were teens, told her jokes about men who fell out of trees raking leaves, told only sweet memories, climbing 7000 feet of slow switchbacks, past meadows rocketed by the flaming tongues of California poppies, desert boulders cracked by eons of sunstroke and wind, past lizard, coyote, hummingbird whir and hawk, past waxy prickly pear and ocotillo bloom up finally to Ponderosa pines and junipers, all the way to the top of Mt. Lemmon, where the hoop of her dusky breath slowed enough for her to leap clean through.

# FIGHTING THE COLD

Look at these hands, purpled by May's final
winter slap, wrinkled as rice paper, chilled
from eating cottage cheese and wind
that knifes through branches like a rapist
        through lace.  My clipped thumbnail is
my dad's aurora borealis of pale eggplant and tangerine,
Grandma's small fingers, tiny moons
white-rimmed and hard as the knuckle on a ghost.
Some days I believe I will never warm up.
Love has tucked its laughter behind metal clouds,
inside the entities of crystalline snow.
This morning, thinking it spring, I wrapped
the cord around the electric heater,
stowed it deep in the stone basement.

Oh stupid faith, like my friend said, I have a face
that feeds on false hope.  Now falling
low as my blood pressure
late winter clouds razor the tips of new aspen
leaves, frost sweet alyssum and bleeding hearts.
But this poem is supposed to be about my hands
and the way they drop spoons when they're cold,
the way they can't hold their own warmth
and sometimes hurt so bad the cartilage screams.
My mother said warm heart, but I know
it's just bad circulation, the unwillingness of the heart
wounded too often to share a gush of new blood.

I remember the way my father's hand
clawed, middle finger drawn tight as a bowstring
to the palm by the stiff sinew, his inflexible will
while grandma's remained graceful, young as green flames.

Before it's too late and my fingers lock
around their empty globe of air,  they must learn
the fine art of fire, to consume,
be consumed.

# WILDFLOWERS

*For Anna Petroska Jackinchuk (1894–1983)*


I


I arrange cornflowers, brown-eyed Susans,
roadside purple rockets--
decades since you taught me their names.
        You said wind scoured words from your head,
blowing stronger each year.

Grandma, how completely your stories flew me
to the old country, red poppies and mountains
blue as aging veins, cures boiled from mushrooms,
        and the times, coming home late, you hid
in river willows
        spying on a gypsy camp.
Dreaming of perfect love, you hugged your knees against
the cold and rocked
to balalaikas
and guitars carved from tongues of fire,
dancing like icons in your mother's bedroom.

That dark pulse caught you early
when, instead of capping beer in the family brewery,
you climbed onto blocks of straw-covered ice
and twirled until you flipped
head-first to the skidding floor.
Unconscious days you dreamed
you were a wren tossed inside a storm.
When you woke, the wind began.

Did you think it was penance
that your mother sent you alone

and knowing no English
to be saved by America?
          Your sole welcome to Ellis Island
were gusting Atlantic waves and a cousin
who sold you to a sweat shop.


II


In Philadelphia you rolled cigars
then fled, strange wren, to sing
and dance in carnivals until you saw Grandfather's
fire-black eyes in his charmed face.
High-stepping, he was
your fairy tale Russian prince.

Remember yellow roses, amethyst
lilacs, kiss-me-over-the-garden-gate?
Their petals held no alien voice
but became the fluid language
you composed into a garden
when Grandfather betrayed
his promises of faith and lace.

Even as you planted the Peace Rose,
packing black soil around its waxy trunk,
he bootlegged whiskey from Canada,
bought long black sedans
and pearl-studded suits to win
women whose gorgeous faces
you weeded from nightmares.

His manic laughter was prohibition
that kept you at the stove over borscht,
babka, duck blood soup.
                    How you hated to sing

and dance for his Purple Gang friends.
That bloody mob stuffed
the false walls of your house
with whiskey and bathtub gin, used your sons
as mannequins to foil police.

My favorite story is the final time
that Grandfather met you
at the front door, taut leather strap
slapping his palm as you led your kids
back from the Saturday matinee.

Over the porch rail you shattered
a milk bottle, whispering
          *No sir, Mister, now things must change.*

Broken glass striping his throat, he
dropped the belt, and from that day
you passed untouched.
You took in bushels of laundry,
mopped rich oak floors so you could buy
bread with your independent coins.
By that sweet rebellion
your children were fed.

Bullets tore the roots from your dreams
those long months Grandfather was shuttled
to prison for a murder no one could prove.
          On his last parole he beat
your oldest son, my father, then
backhanded him through the bleeding porch door.

His furious screams could not order
his son back to the terrified house.

Hours before you got off work
Grandfather locked the kitchen doors,
blew out the pilot,
and suffocated the bloom of his
sorrow in your stove.


III


Is it any surprise you warned me
about men?  Like all warriors,
you stood your own ground, even
the time your second husband was so drunk
he couldn't recall
how whiskey drove anger
        when he split the kitchen table top
with a cleaver meant for you.
        Mowing the lawn he cut
the plush tongues of snapdragons,
fragile moss rose,
snow-on-the-mountain,
cursing stems and petals clogging his blades.

Complaints were as foreign as I would become to you.
Memorizing your hands, weightless
and resilient as bird bones,
I came to say goodbye.
You pointed to the magnolia opening the yard
with blossoms healing as your absolute laughter.
        So far north, you marveled
it survived so many winters
when hardier plants died.

I told you I was flying to mountains
I'd never seen, knowing
I had to cultivate other ground.

I tried to talk you into coming along
but you repeated,
>  *Wildflowers can't be transplanted.*
>  *I want to die in my own house.*

Grandma, you loved best
dark petals,
>            black marooned roses,
cinnamon deep azaleas.
The richest you fixed in my hair.
I still can't turn from your blue eyes
that tend a garden I could own.

There is no sound as loud as
this passing when you waved through the screen,
>  *I'll see you in the clouds*
>  *when the wind stops.*

# LIGHT IS THE KNIFE

*For Claude Bailey*


that carves the spines of mountains, inescapable
as breath or killer bees.  Across town, Claude is dying
and we don't know what to say or do except remember
before cancer  and the wheelchair, his love sonnets
hand-written to his journalist wife in a world blurred
by high speed wireless, inside traders, plastic diapers
            and bustiers of explosive devices.
Our friend Claude believes in roses and carefully dicing
onions into caviar, believes in the color of champagne.
Did I mention he paints from dreams?
He teaches us not to bury our hearts too early
but to stop rush hour and watch light
reshape the world.  How can we stop holding him,
who becomes lucent as nacre, miraculous
as a star whose brightest burst of flame
seals its own destruction?

# FLYING THROUGH THUNDER

*for John Uschuk and Galway Kinnell*

I

From expectant sunflowers, mountain
blue birds, western meadowlarks
and the melancholy shadows of their songs in sage,
from the spin and groan of the planet
we roar up, bucking through
the blue fury of thunderheads
on our final leg home.

The small turbo prop pitches
toward glacial peaks, saints gleaming
in the numen of autumn sun, while the pilot
warns us that it will be a rough flight.
As if we didn't know, caroming
on the backs of jet stream storms, that
there are few smooth flights, as if we don't read
headlines that daily explode the world.

Below us, dump trucks erect a Denver landfill
into the shape of a Mayan temple
burying the relics of our excess
while lightning cracks its knuckles
on the Front Range and thunder
rattles the thin skin of this twin engine plane
shaking us from our loneliness.
Between bellicose clouds jut
sheer curtains of light.

In this space that freezes our imaginations
we bounce then drop through

air pockets rough as alcoholic fists,
dry sockets of turbulence.


## II

I have no choice but to release any illusion
of control, break my white-knuckled grip
on steel armrests that would splinter on impact
against rock crags that never learned my name.

In the row ahead of me the carefully coifed woman
checks her lipstick as a baby screams
and I wonder at vanity pitching
fragile as a cocoon 20,000 feet above tree line.

I think of the passion of poets
holding their hearts like worn ball caps
in their bruised hands, defying
the spiked teeth of hungry gods
swallowing truth whole before they eat them alive.


## III

Even the stocky steward wipes sweat
from his forehead, groans as if he's giving birth
when we yaw half-over, pushed
by stratospheric gusts we are blind to.

I remember the way my stomach dropped
as a child pumping my swing higher,
pretending I was a pilot bombing enemies,
pretending I wasn't afraid.
At the acme of my pendulum, the swing set ground
against its cement feet, threatening

to slingshot me into space, and my brother
dared me to jump.  His green eyes
were wild as a cougar's, voice screeching
with the blood of pretend death, hands
itching to let go of the chains.  And, he did.

*Bomb's away!  We're hit. Jump. Jump.*
*We're on fire! Jump!*


How could I refuse the catapult
out of that careening or forsee
that in a few years, my brother would be
drafted to paratrooper school,
to ruin his young knees
when he landed just off the training mark
preparing for Vietnam?
When the army found out he attended rallies,
preached peace, he
was shipped to Da Nang, to dousings
with Agent Orange, to the burning
of village peoples, to daily mortar attacks
and sniper fire he still fights.

Leaping from the swing's apogee, what
I savored most was fear's pure torch
scalding my body as it arced, suspended
before the plunge, that moment
                    gravity kicked in, and I knew
what real death would feel like,
hanging a long breath in space
astonished at the constellation of my life
coming into exquisite focus—family,
friends, ambition, anger, even love--before everything
like a billowing parachute
dropped away.

IV

Now as the plane lunges, engines
steady above the Continental Divide,
I regard razor backed ridges
older than memory, vaster
than scars.  They comfort me

in their lack of pity, their indifference
to our cares.  Perhaps this is
all I need to know.  It is not until
we begin to fall that we
learn how sweet the burst
                         of ecstasy, the
release.

# ACKNOWLEDGMENTS

## Journals

*Another Chicago Magazine:* The Horseman of the Crass and Vulnerable
    Word
*Asheville Poetry Review:* We Thought No One Could See Us
*Beloit Poetry Journal:* Sunday News on the Rez
*Eyewear* (London): The Horseman of the Crass and Vulnerable Word
*Future Cycle:* Flying Through Thunder
*Iris:* Self Help Manual
*Isotrope:* Bushwacked: Notes on Global Warming
*Mountain Gazette:* Climbing Down Engineer Mountain and
    Christmas Dawn
*Neidergasse:* Nothing But Southern and 80th Birthday
*Nimrod:* A Dream, My Child
*Out of Line:* North Carolina Spring Meditation
*Pequod:* With Its Toll of Char
*Peregrine:* In the Egyptian Rooms
*PIF:* Adult Orthodontics, Hit and Run, and Bell Note
*Poetry:* Meditations Beside Kootenai Creek
*Poetry Miscellany:* Money Can't Buy You
*Rattapallax:* Fighting the Cold
*Santa Fe Literary Journal:* White Moths
*Southeastern Review:* Leaving Chattanooga
*Sow's Ear:* Motorcycle Accident (Semi-finalist in the *Sow's Ear*
    Poetry Contest)
*Village Rambler:* A Small Ode to Wine (Struga Poetry Prize; Published
    also in Macedonia, translated by Bogomil Gjuzel)
*Zone:* Wildflowers

## Anthologies

*Bridges: Poets of the Hudson Valley:* With Its Toll of Char
*Only in Her Shoes:* Wildflowers
*Sourcebooks Calendar:* White Moths, Light is the Knife, and Radha
    Longs for the Lion

My gratitude goes to my dear friend, Joy Harjo, with whom
I've shared poetry, dreams and laughter for nearly 25 years, to the
late Mary Ann Campau and to Emilie George for their invaluable

help in proofing parts of the text. David Appelbaum and Cod Hill Press were kind enough to publish the chapbook, *Heartbeats In Stones*, in which some of the poems in this manuscript appeared. And how could I live without those friends and family who have been there for me: Kate Bell, Holly & Frank Bergon, Robert Olen Butler, Howie Faerstein, Teri Hairston, Terry Harvey, Cynthia Hogue, Rick Jackson, Richard Katrovas, Willie James King, Charlotte Lowe, Bill and Cindy Luvaas, Naomi Shihab Nye, Jennifer Lorca Root, Kasia Sokol, Kevin Watson, my siblings, my Aunt Olga, and all my cousins, nephews and nieces. *Un mil gracias* to Bryce Milligan, publisher of Wings Press, who continues to have faith in my work and who is one of American poetry's most unselfish gatekeepers. I am humbled and grateful for the presence in my life of my husband and one of the finest poets I know, William Pitt Root, whose love has made so many of these poems possible.

*Pamela Uschuk,*
*kayaking the chill waters of Vallecito Reservoir*
*at 8,000 feet in the Southwestern Rockies.*

# ABOUT THE AUTHOR

Called by *The Bloomsbury Review* "one of the most insightful and spirited poets today," Pamela Uschuk is the author of four volumes of poetry: the award-winning *Finding Peaches in the Desert, One-Legged Dancer, Scattered Risks* (all published by Wings Press) and *Without the Comfort of Stars* (Sampark Press, New Delhi and London). *Scattered Risks* was nominated for both a Pulitzer Prize and the 2005 Zacharias Poetry Award (nomination by *Ploughshares*). Joy Harjo and other musicians joined Uschuk on a CD of *Finding Peaches.* The author of numerous chapbooks, her work has appeared in well over two hundred fifty journals and anthologies, including *Agni Review, Calyx, Future Cycles, Nimrod, Parabola, Parnassus Review, Pequod, Ploughshares, Poetry, O Taste and See, 48 Younger American Poets*, etc.

Uschuk's literary prizes include the Struga International Poetry Prize, the Dorothy Daniels Writing Award from the National League of American PEN Women, the 2001 Literature Award from the Tucson/Pima Arts Council for *Finding Peaches in the Desert,* The King's English Prize, as well as awards from the Chester H. Jones Foundation, *Iris, Ascent, Sandhills Review,* and Amnesty International. Her work has been translated into a dozen languages, including Albanian, Bulgarian, Czech, Spanish, French, German, Korean, Macedonian, Swedish, Russian, and Slovak.

She has been a featured writer at the American Center in New Delhi, India, the Prague Summer Workshops, the University of Pisa, International Poetry Festivals in Malmö, Sweden and Struga, Macedonia, the British School in Pisa, Italy, Vilenica in Slovenia, Split This Rock, Gemini Ink Writers Festival, the Meacham Writers Conference, the Book Marks Book Fair, the Scandinavian Book Fair, the Deep South Writers Conference, the Universities of Arizona, New Mexico, Montana, Tennessee, Lund, Gothenberg (Sweden), Oregon, Montana State, Colorado State and California State Universities, New York University, Juilliard, Hunter College, Vassar College, SUNY New Paltz, and numerous colleges and book stores.

Uschuk has taught creative writing at Marist College, Pacific Lutheran University, Fort Lewis College, the University of Arizona's Poetry Center and Salem College. She also spent many years traveling to teach creative writing to Native American students on the Salish, Sioux, Assiniboine, Flathead, Northern Cheyenne, Blackfeet, Crow, Tohono O'odham and Yaqui reservations in Montana and Arizona. Before moving back to Colorado, Uschuk was the Director of the Center for Women Writers at Salem College, where she has also taught Creative Writing. Editor-In-Chief of the literary magazine, *Cutthroat: A Journal of the Arts,* she is a professor of Creative Writing at Fort Lewis College in Durango, Colorado. She makes her home with the writer William Pitt Root, their two dogs, Happy and Zazu, and the queen of cats, Sadie.

## CRITICAL PRAISE FOR EARLIER WORKS BY PAMELA USCHUK:

"These poems make a sensual garden. The gifts of the earth can be found here: from peaches to lizards to rich earth that soaks up the spilled blood of history. There is the promise of rain and the sky filled with spirits of those we become. There is singing in this garden, and though it might be the end of the world, a new world is coming into view, just over the horizon of these poems."

– Joy Harjo

"These poems are breathtaking, a triumph of language and spirit. . . . This book is a call to contemplation and action, celebration and a righteous anger that can transform the world we inhabit."

– Demetria Martínez

Whether she writes of the sexy quiet of marriage . . . or the lacerating political rage that bursts out of many of these pages, Uschuk maintains the light that burns in her chest. All the landscapes here – from the desert's rumpled floor to the poet's own bed to the torture chambers of Chile – are alive and vivid with this light. The book is long overdue."

– Luis Urrea

"She is a skilled traveler in dry lands, a knowing observer of animal and human ways, gifted with a sure eye and the master of an idiom charged with meaning and feeling. . . . *Finding Peaches in the Desert* is a sturdy and striking collection that merits a wide audience."

– *Parabola*

*Colophon*

This first edition of *Crazy Love*, by Pamela Uschuk, has been printed on 70 pound paper containing fifty percent recycled fiber. Titles have been set in Herculanum type, the text is in Adobe Caslon type. All Wings Press books are designed and produced by Bryce Milligan.

On-line catalogue and ordering:
www.wingspress.com

Wings Press titles are distributed
to the trade by the
Independent Publishers Group
www.ipgbook.com
and in Europe by
www.gazellebookservices.co.uk